WHY DO I POO?

BY KIRSTY HOLMES

THE SECRET BOOK COMPANY

©2019
The Secret Book Company
King's Lynn
Norfolk PE30 4LS

All rights reserved.
Printed in Malaysia.

A catalogue record for this
book is available from the
British Library.

ISBN: 978-1-78998-056-1

Written by:
Kirsty Holmes

Edited by:
Holly Duhig

Designed by:
Danielle Rippengill

All facts, statistics, web addresses and URLs in this book were verified as valid and accurate at time of writing.
No responsibility for any changes to external websites or references can be accepted by either the author or publisher.

WHY DO I POO?

CONTENTS

Words that look like **this** can be found in the glossary on page 24.

DO YOU NEED THE LOO?

Birds do it, bears do it, mice that live under the stairs do it… everybody poos! But have you ever wondered how? What about why? Where does poo come from?

And where does it go?

Every day, we eat and drink. Our bodies are like clever factories – they take the good stuff out of your food, and get rid of what's left as poo (and wee)!

FOOD GOES IN

All people and animals need to eat. Food gives us **nutrients** that all living things need to survive – and we need lots of different nutrients every day.

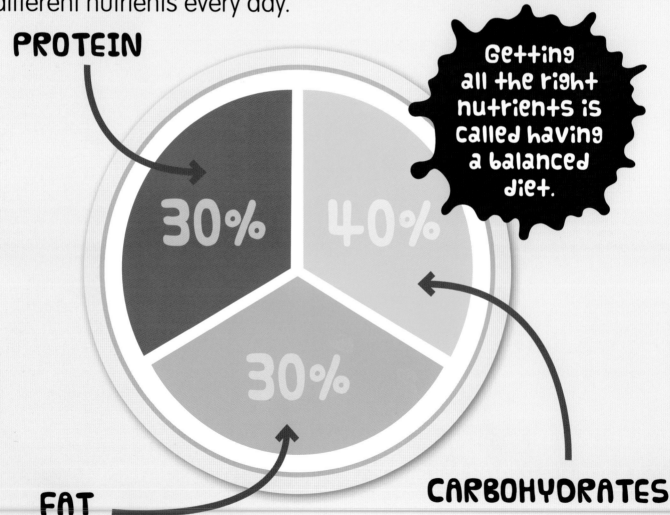

PROTEIN

30%

40%

30%

FAT

CARBOHYDRATES

Getting all the right nutrients is called having a balanced diet.

Our bodies have very clever **systems** to help us get these nutrients out of our food, and to the parts of our bodies that need them.

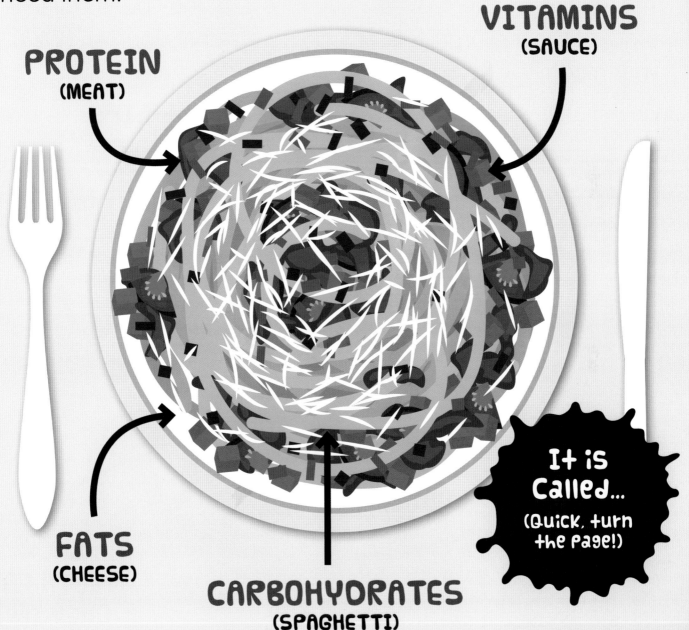

PROTEIN
(MEAT)

VITAMINS
(SAUCE)

FATS
(CHEESE)

CARBOHYORATES
(SPAGHETTI)

It is Called...
(Quick, turn the page!)

THE DIGESTIVE SYSTEM

The digestive system is made up of lots of body parts called organs. The first organs your food meets on its journey are in your mouth.

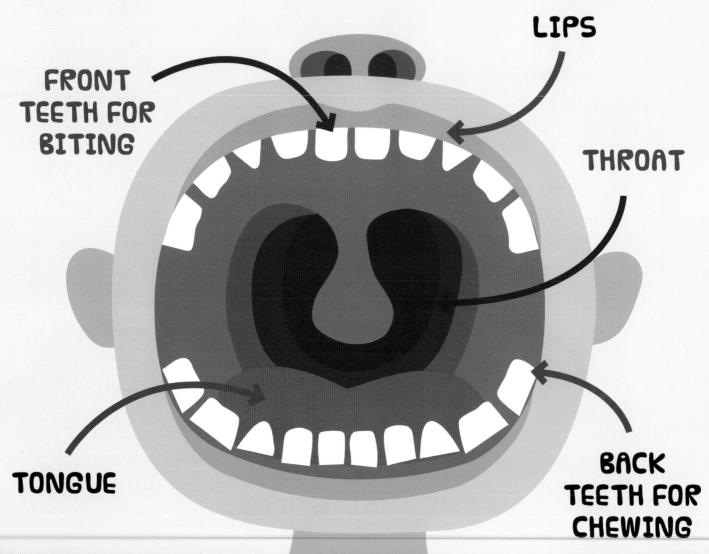

LIPS

FRONT TEETH FOR BITING

THROAT

TONGUE

BACK TEETH FOR CHEWING

The first thing you need to do to get all those nutrients out of your food is to chew it up, until it is mushy enough to swallow.

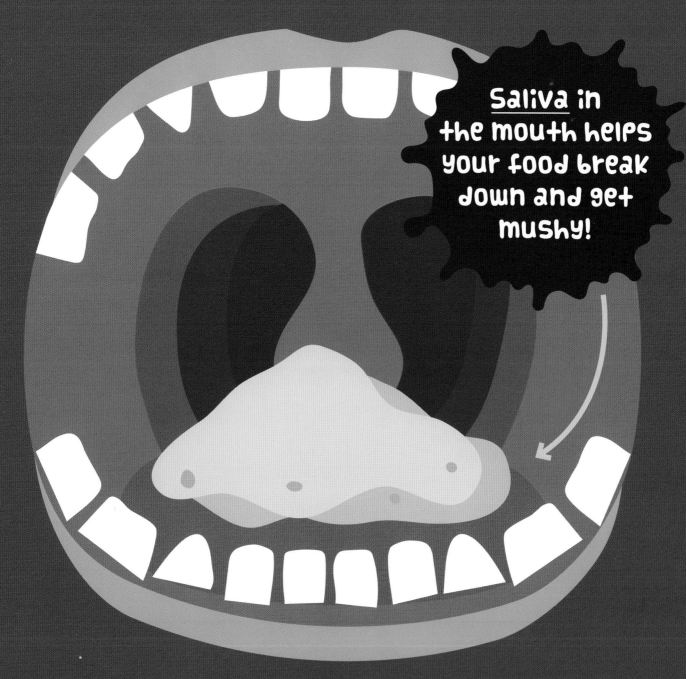

Saliva in the mouth helps your food break down and get mushy!

JOURNEY OF A POO

HOW DOES A PIZZA BECOME A POO?

STEP 1:
You eat the food, chew it up in your **MOUTH**, and swallow it.

STEP 2:
Food travels down the **OESOPHAGUS** — special muscles push and squeeze it down, like a tube of toothpaste!

STEP 3:
The food sits in your **STOMACH** for about four hours! Special **enzymes** break the food into nutrients our body can use.

STEP 5: ... the **LARGE INTESTINE**, where the last nutrients are removed and the waste is squashed into...

STEP 6: POO!

STEP 4: In the **SMALL INTESTINE**, the nutrients are absorbed into the body and the waste is pushed into...

POO COMES OUT

HIGH FIBRE FOOD

Fibre is really good for your digestion. Good **bacteria** living in your gut like to eat it, and it helps your poo come out more easily.

Once your body has taken all the nutrients out of your food, there is usually some stuff left over that can't be digested. This is the waste matter, and it's mostly made of fibre.

Fibre makes up part of your poo. The rest is made of water, dead bacteria (which is what makes it smelly!) and **mucus**.

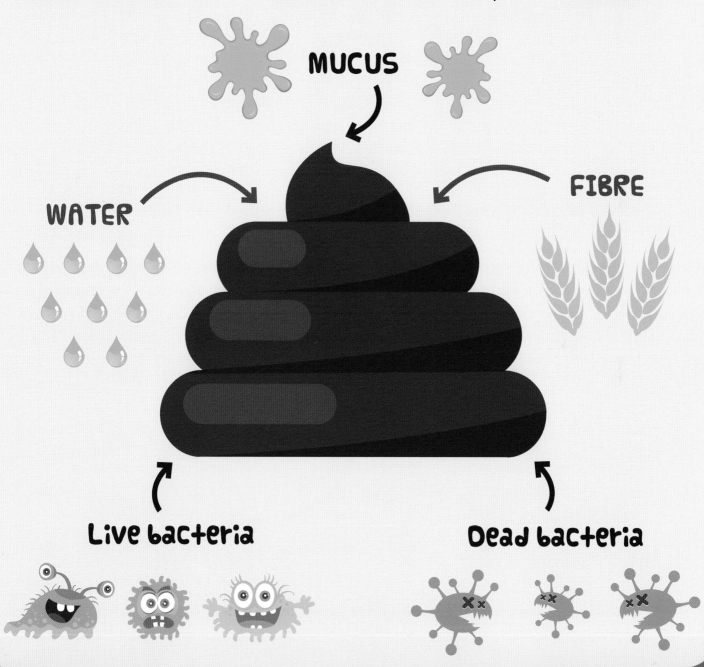

MUCUS

WATER

FIBRE

Live bacteria

Dead bacteria

WEE AND WIND

Your poo isn't the only waste product you make.

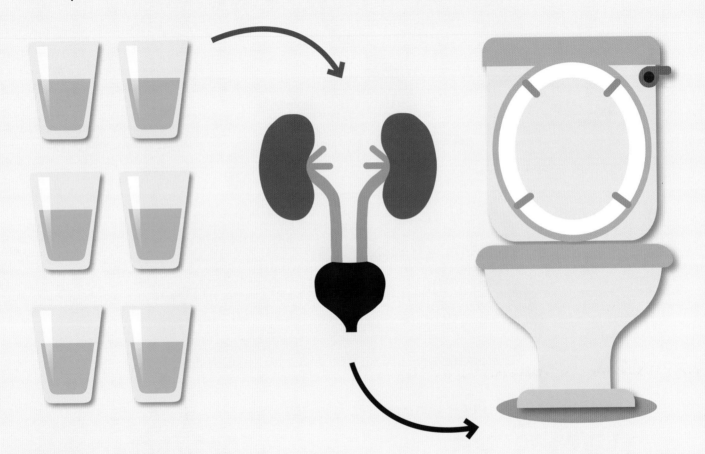

Wee

Your wee, also called urine, is the waste liquid made by a pair of organs called the kidneys, which clean out your blood.

Wind

When you eat, you swallow some air with your food. Friendly bacteria in your gut also make **gas** as they break down your food. So… well, there are lots of names for this that are too rude for this book so we'll say… you pass wind.

This air and gas has got to get out again or you'd explode!

UPSET TUMMIES

It's a poo-mergency!

If you can't do a poo at all, or your poo is very hard and hurts, this is called constipation **(SAY: CON-STI-PAY-SHUN)**.

Constipation can give you a stomach ache.

If you need to go very **<u>urgently</u>**, and your poo is very watery and thin, this is called diarrhoea **(SAY: DIE-A-REE-AH).**

Both constipation and diarrhoea can be caused by lots of things. Tell the grown-up who looks after you if you have either of these and they will give you some medicine to help.

RATE YOUR POO!

Poo comes in lots of different shapes and sizes, and even colours! We can tell a lot about our health from our poo. Let's see what we can find out...

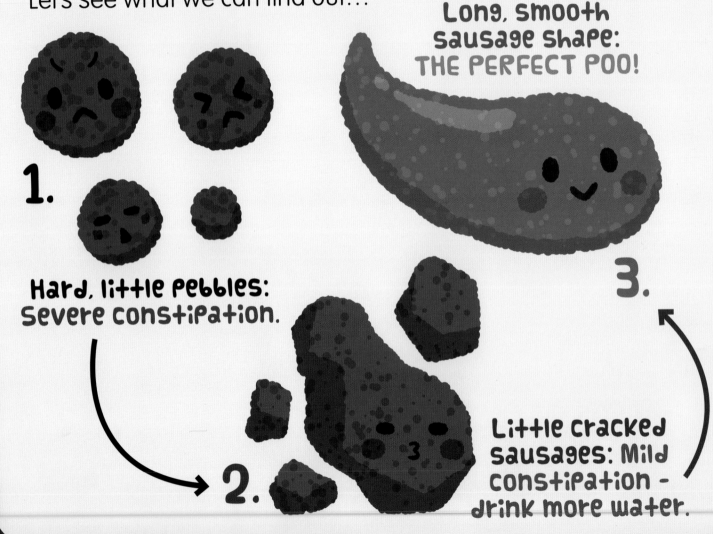

Long, smooth sausage shape: THE PERFECT POO!

1.

Hard, little pebbles: Severe constipation.

2.

3.

Little cracked sausages: Mild constipation - drink more water.

4.

Soft blobs: Your diet needs more fibre to hold your poo together.

Don't touch your poo, and always wash your hands after going to the toilet!

5.

Mushy and squishy: Mild diarrhoea.

6.

Liquid: Severe diarrhoea.

This is called the Bristol Stool Scale. Stool is a word doctors use for poo!

SUPER POOPERS!

Poo Power!

Poo gives off methane, a gas which can be burned to produce energy and power our homes!

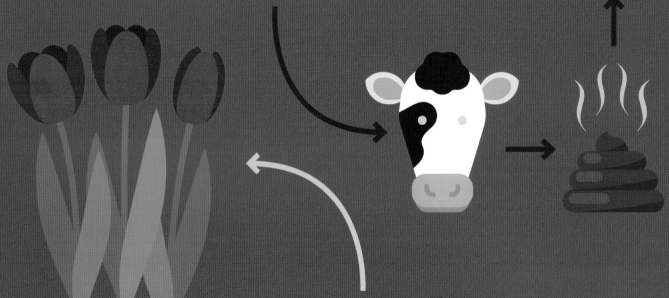

Grow your Own!

Animal poo is a natural **<u>fertiliser</u>** that helps plants to grow.

Drive a Bus!

→

In 2014, the first poo-powered bus hit the streets of the UK. It uses human waste to create methane gas, and runs on the number 2 route.

Poo Paper!

Poo has a lot of fibre in it, so in some places it's made into paper! Elephant poo, sheep poo… even panda poo!

WHOSE POO?

Can you match the poo to the pooper in this stinky quiz?

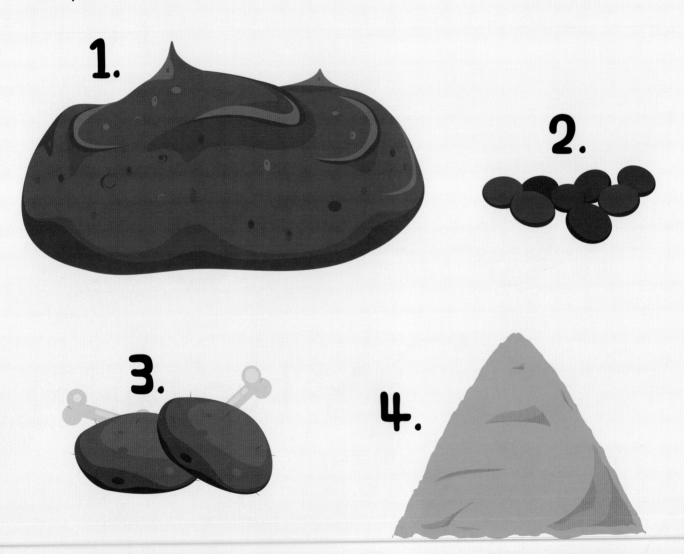

1.

2.

3.

4.

Rats sometimes eat their own Poo! (Don't do this! Yuck!)

Parrot fish eat so much coral that they poo out sand!

Owl poo is called a pellet and we can find out a lot about the owl's <u>prey</u> by looking inside for bones!

Elephants can make between 35 and 135 kilograms of poo a day!

Answers: Poo 1: Elephant; Poo 2: Rat; Poo 3: Owl; Poo 4: Parrot fish.

23

GLOSSARY

bacteria   tiny living things, which are too small to see

enzymes   things made by living things that help the body in lots of ways, such as by breaking down food

fertiliser   things added to crops that help them to grow

fibre   the tough part of a plant that can't be digested

gas   a thing that is like air, which spreads out to fill any space available

mucus   a slimy substance that helps to protect and lubricate certain parts of the human body

nutrients   natural things that people need to grow and stay healthy

prey   animals that are hunted by other animals for food

saliva   the liquid made in the mouth to help with digestion and tasting

systems   sets of things that work together to do specific jobs

urgently   needing immediate action or attention

INDEX

24